Table of Contents

DEDICATION

This book is dedicated to my late mother, Rita A. Alexander; she was more than just a mother. A child's first impression of God's love is a mother's love. Her sacrifices for her kids went unwavering. I still draw from the lessons I learned from you. You were always there when I needed a voice of reason. You believed in me when I didn't believe in myself...I love you always.

ACKNOWLEDGMENT

First and foremost, thank You, God, for Your unfailing love, grace, and mercy. To my wife, my best friend, Denise, who always encourages and inspires me to be all that God has destined for me. My love for you is indescribable.

To our four children - Emmanuel, Da'Shun, Alex, and Rileigh, you are my joy and motivation. You all have my heart! I love and believe in you all, and I am so proud of you all. Always remember Philippians 4:13, "You can do ALL things through Christ who strengthens you."

To my brothers: Vidal Alexander, you took on a huge role at such a young age. I appreciate you every day for your love, motivation, and inspiration during my times of defeat. You were always a hero to me, and I still look up to you till this day. Shaquille Sturgill, you made me better at an early age. I appreciate your words of encouragement, and I hope I made you both proud? I love you guys.

I am grateful to literally thousands of people that I have met for their help and support in life and with this book. There are so many of you to name, from relatives, mentors to brothers and sisters in arms. So, I leave you with these two words. Thank You! I pray this book will bless you and all who read it.

Stay Blessed!

The Overview

Over the years, I became aware of a large decrease in leaders. I noticed managers were taking over due to the high demands of organizations. A lot of people became cookie cutters when it came to their leadership and forgot the importance behind it. The content of this book is aimed at aligning leaders to enhance themselves and their teams' ability to critically & creatively think; synergize expertise and teaching to assist leaders with empowering, goal setting, effectively communicate, team building and operate effortlessly regardless of environment or condition, with confidence and exceptional knowledge.

This book is a handbook to help unlock the leadership potential we have all been blessed with. I truly believe everything rises and falls on leadership. Leaders are needed everywhere, in families, schools, churches and organizations. The most important part of a phone is the charger. If the charger does not work, the phone is inoperable. Let me break this down for you; the leader is the charger, and the employees are the phones.

I say that to note that everyone has to be connected to some source of authority. For organizations, the lack of people possessing leadership traits causes a loss in cost. Companies have to invest in their workers if they expect the moral to increase and managers to not misuse their power. I believe it is a leader's responsibility to project the inspiration and mold the business culture.

This book is for "ALL" leaders striving to maximize their employee's potential through effective leadership. It's also for those looking to become better leaders to maximize their organization's potential and those that lost sight due to the high demands.

Introduction

First, a Warning:

L et me make something crystal clear before we go any further.

The ideas and strategies revealed in this book are only for people who are willing to look at leadership from a different point of view, beyond being just a manager.

This book will only benefit people willing to acknowledge that there are plenty of leadership opportunities.

Now, I realize this may sound strange for a "Warning"; however, it's incredibly important!

What if I tell you, "You're losing generous amounts of money by failing to be an effective leader?" What if I tell you, "You cost your company financially by failing to invest in the leaders in your organization?"

This book details seven different attributes I've personally used over the past 15 years in maintaining the success of my organization.

This book is a quick and easy read. A complete front to back reading can be accomplished over the course of a weekend or within a few weeks. It's a "Go-To" reference! There's no technical language, and the methods are spelled out in the simplest terms.

Furthermore, I illustrate with biblical studies and examples from my personal experiences. The reader is able to see, first-hand, how it works and the impressive results the system provides.

You'll immediately "recognize" the entire system I've personally used to permanently "upgrade" my leadership strategies and empower future generations of leaders.

"The single biggest way to impact an organization is to focus on leadership development. There is almost no limit to the potential of an organization that recruits good people, raises them up as leaders and continually develops them."

-John Maxwel

Chapter 1

Becoming A Leader

YOU! have tremendous potential to become a leader. Perhaps, no one has ever motivated you to find it. Genesis 1:26-28 tells us that we, as humans, are created in His likeness and image. We are accountable to Him because He gave us the authority to rule over the earth. But, to rule or lead, we must first discover our unique purpose. I was just a kid from one of the most intangible cities in the United States. I joined the military to get away from my environment, a low-income single-parent home on the south side of Columbus better known as Killumbus. Chances of becoming a victim of violent crime are 1 in 125 in a population of 194,000.

The odds were stacked against my siblings and I. By the age of 13, I had joined a gang, doing drugs, alcohol and seen a dead body. I never had any intention of becoming a leader.

I joined the military because of job security and because everyone in my family did it.

For my first eight years of the Army, I considered myself to be a follower that transitioned to a manager of soldiers. I did not think I had what it took to become a leader. I was placed in leadership positions but did not know what my obligation was in leadership. It wasn't until 2011 that I realized I had leadership potential. It was then that I accepted the challenge. I had awakened a sleeping giant, the undiscovered leader, and strived to become a positive influence.

Over the next decade, I was committed to becoming an effective leader through extensive military training and reading multiple books from Stephen Covey, John Maxwell, Simon Sinek, and the late Dr. Myles Munroe, obtaining my Bachelor of Science in Organizational Leadership from CSU and becoming an honorary member of the NSLS (National Society of Leadership and Success).

I was in charge of multiple organizations with 50 -100+ soldiers under my charge. I was not always successful, but I never quit following my purpose. Over time, I have empowered a ton of people by helping them reach their goals, both personally and professionally. I inspired people more and more to fulfill their obligations. I wanted to show everyone what I encountered; that it was not the cards that you are dealt, but how you are playing your cards.

How many of you feel that you have been passed over for promotion? That you could lead better than those in leadership positions? Let me tell you, don't put your head down and just work hard. Pick your head up and understand what it takes to get promoted. But just remember that the title or position does not guarantee execution or productivity.

Great leaders have a foundation of self-purpose, and they continue to learn every day. You cannot become complacent. Leadership is like a muscle; if you want to become stronger, you have to train constantly. When you workout for one day, do you see a change in your body?

No! You do not. The same rules apply to leadership. You do not become a leader overnight. It takes what I call the 3-D effect.

What is the 3-D effect, you may ask? It's the quality of being three-dimensional by using Discipline, Dedication and Determination. Leadership is critical in all organizations to maximize efficiency and to reach the corporation's goals. Without leaders, teams become disorganized, ineffective, and disinterested.

Leaders have great *discipline,* and they want to inspire others to follow the same path. They build the values and behaviors of a team. Ask yourself, do you want average re-sults or extraordinary results? Such skills and qualities are really important not only in the workplace but in our daily lives. Holding ourselves accountable for our action takes a lot of self-love and willpower.

Leaders are *dedicated* to their charge. They are able to harness everyone's energy and ability for the good of the team. Without a leader, there isn't a standard to follow, and team integrity eventually erodes. Ask yourself, do you want to achieve something truly amazing? Relationships, business, health, or anything else?

The ***determined*** leaders are the ones with emotional intelligence and strength. When you find this leader that desires to get the job done and has characteristics such as initiative, persistence, dominance, and drive, ask what are you hungry for? What brings you alive? It is all about finding your passion.

You know, their passion for achieving a noble goal coupled with a calculated plan, equals success. It's never crowded going the extra mile. It takes these three words, Dedication, Determination and Discipline to get there. Leadership is more than hard work; it is nonstop work. Few people stick it out to get world-class results. It's not always easy, but it is always worth it.

Chapter 2

Influence

The capacity to affect the character, development, or behavior of someone or something, or the effect itself. Influence is the key to being successful in leadership.

Titus 2:7 reads, "Show yourself in all respects to be a model of good works, and in your teaching show integrity, dignity".

When I was an AIT Platoon Sergeant at Fort Jackson, South Carolina, we would welcome new warriors with a newcomer's brief. During my brief, I would introduce myself and tell them the significance of them joining and being part of the one percent.

I would tell them they are part of a team that would sacrifice more for their well-being greater than some of their friends they grew up with. I would end by letting them know that I do not train soldiers; I train future leaders. Also, that for the next twelve weeks and one day, I would be the closest thing they have to a parent.

As a successful leader, you have to invest strongly in each member of the team. You have to build trust but verify, share your passion, and give them something to believe in. It's what we call in the Army, "make them drink the kool-aid". You have to know your target audience in your approach. You, as the leader, can be more effective by the way you approach your employees.

For example, as a parent with multiple kids like myself, my kids are all different, and I cannot approach them the same. One day, I told my three boys to clean their rooms; when I went to check how things are going, one of my sons told me his room was clean before I even mentioned it. Another one was in the middle of cleaning his when I came to check. The third one was lying in bed on his phone, with his room still dirty. As the head of my household, it is my responsibility to make sure my house has good order and discipline.

So, I asked my son if he heard me when I told them they needed to clean their rooms. He said, "yes, sir." I asked him what is preventing him from making that happen? He said, "I thought you meant sometime today, not right now." Now, the First Sergeant in me wanted to give him the knife hand and put him in the front lean and rest. But, as his father, I realized he needed guidance and encouragement, unlike his brothers. Once he finished, I told him thank you and that he did a great job.

I never had an issue the next time I told him to clean his room. I gave this example to say that all your employees are diverse, and you cannot approach them the same. We, as the leader, can sometimes get frustrated dealing with these workers that do not execute a task when told. I am here to say that some employees need more influence than others. Some members are self-motivated, some are easy to communicate with and some need a little more encouraging and nourishment to get the job done. This is your obligation as the leader to develop. I understand that, at times, this can be difficult due to corporate demands. This is where emotional intelligence needs to be utilized. We will talk more about emotional intelligence in the following chapters.

It is undeniable that Super Bowl Champion, Russell Wilson of the Seattle Seahawks, is one of the most resilient football players of all time. Has it ever crossed your mind, "Why?" Well...He understands what his responsibility is as the leader of the team. He knows that everyone has a specific job and that he has to influence them.

He knows it's his responsibility to convince other players to be the best at their positions. Russell persuades his players to drink the kool-aid. He knows you cannot just talk about it; you have to be about it.

If you're striving to be an influence on your employees or team, I strongly encourage that you become the example that you want to follow. Talent will get you in the door, but your character will keep you in the room.

Chapter 3

Servant Leadership

The first step in becoming an effective leader is being a follower. The most astonishing person known to man established a huge degree of servant leadership. In John 13 of the Bible, Jesus washed the feet of His disciples. In Luke 22:27, He spoke of who is greater, the one who sits at the table or the one who serves?

During my time as a First Sergeant, I wrote on my white-board, "It's Not About You." I would look at this every day to remind myself exactly that because I was there to serve the people, not the other way around. If it weren't for the leaders and soldiers under my charge, I would not be able to accomplish any mission.

The Army value, "Selfless Service" stands out because it wasn't about the accolades or recognition from higher echelons, it was about empowering and the camaraderie of the team. The success of any organization lies within the team. When the leader places the needs of the employees above their own to achieve a common goal, the results are impeccable. They must be able to set their own ego aside and realize that without their team of employees, no one can be successful.

Servant leadership focuses on the acts of the leader with the tools and methods they use to grow and develop their team. Taking the time to counsel and identify your employees' strengths and shortcomings aid employees' performance at times; even being beside them as they face challenges helps too. It is a leader's responsibility to guide their followers on the right path.

You, as the leader, must level the success of the task with how you treat and care for your employees. A leader should strive to develop relationships and even friendships with their employees and deliver feedback when possible. A good leader knows that a chain is only as strong as its weakest link, so everyone benefits when every employee is encouraged, mentored, and motivated.

Sometimes, this may mean you having to share in successes, as well as failures. Every goal set and worked on together is another stepping stone for the employees as it helps them work toward their ultimate target. Servant leaders are transparent; they are the realest. Being transparent is powerful; a servant leader wants to empower their employees. They look for the ideas and creativity of the team.

Leaders ask questions like, how can I or we become better? They invite feedback and don't mind being vulnerable about the suggestion they receive. Servant leadership is an influence process. As leaders, we sometimes forget our purpose. When in leadership positions, it's not about being in charge, it's about taking care of those in our charge.

Everyone wins when the leader gets better.

Chapter 4

Self-Leadership

Great leadership starts with self-leadership. One of the most important things you will ever do as a leader is to invest in yourself. You cannot fully engage your team or organization to be successful if this does not occur.

It involves working on your skills from the inside out and discovering your purpose. You have to be self-disciplined, making the hard right, and sacrificing pleasure for your purpose. A perfect example is six-time Super Bowl Champion, three-time NFL MVP, Tom Brady. Tom was drafted in the sixth round as the 199 pick to be the backup quarterback.

After being drafted so late, Tom Brady made it his priority to improve in all areas that caused him to be passed over by all 32 teams those five previous rounds. He became the starting quarterback in week two of the 2002 season.

Just in his second season, he led the New England Patri-
ots to their first Super Bowl win and was named MVP of the
game. A self-leader develops and takes responsibility for
their actions. They are self-disciplined, competent and over-
come their weaknesses. You must commit to morals and values to develop your character.

In May 1999, at the age of 19, I donned an Army uniform
and completed my Basic Combat Training at Fort Benning,
GA. I remember being in a shark attack and standing chest-
high to a Drill Sergeant calling me everything but a child of
God.

Over the next nine weeks, I was taught to shoot, move,
communicate, carry a lot of weight, the Army values, structure and become one of the fittest soldiers to support and de-
fend this country.

After my first three years in the military, I was following
suit to the stigma of "I'm a product of my environment." I
was still doing drugs, drinking and getting into fights. I had
broken up with my fiancée, who was pregnant by another
man, received multiple article 15s for my behavior and actions.

Now, after 21 years of military service on active duty,
I'm convinced that experience is the hardest teacher since it
gives the exam before any lessons are taught. The demands
of facing adversity are excruciating and never-ending.

I was constantly trying to figure out ways to develop myself in positive ways that equal prosperity. I became self-mo-

tivated and built myself from within. I gained self-awareness; I grew familiar with my intentions and values. I increased my confidence, as well as being aware of what could keep me from becoming a good leader.

A self-leader has the ability or has learned to have the ability to influence their own thinking, behaviors, and feelings. These individuals guide themselves in positive ways, which is equivalent to success. Leaders never compromise their integrity to gain recognition.

When I took charge of my first organization, every Monday morning before I have accountability formation, I would have soldiers showing up late. I would stop them in their tracks while they are running to get into formation.

I would tell them to get in the front lean and rest, also known as the push-up position. Then ask them why they were late? They would come with excuses after excuses.

I would tell the entire formation excuses does not rhyme with accountability, but responsibility does. It is your responsibility to be here on time, not mine. It is my job as your leader to hold you accountable when you do not show up on time.

God already knows why you're here; you just have to ask Him to reveal His plan and purpose for you to you. In Jeremiah 1:5, the Lord said before you knew the light of day I already knew "ALL" about you. Self-leadership is the foundation of becoming a better leader. Holding ourselves accountable for our action takes a lot of self-love. Knowledge allows us to know what to do, skills gives us the ability to know how to do it, and desire is the motivation to do it.

You have to be committed to your growth and going outside your comfort zone. You are the other half of the equation for your success. The more self-leadership we obtain, the more successful we become. The more successful we become, the more self-leadership we need.

Chapter 5

Emotional Intelligence

I considered myself to be a good leader for a long time. But it wasn't until I was pursuing my Bachelor's in Organizational Leadership that I learned I had a lot more growing to do.

Emotional intelligence, also known as emotional quotient (EQ), is the capacity to be aware of, control, and express one's emotions, and to handle interpersonal relationships judiciously and empathetically. As leaders, we need to be strong in this area. It has been proven that emotional intelligence is more important than technical knowledge.

Without emotional intelligence, we cannot communicate effectively with our team and others. The success of a team or an organization is based on the emotional intelligence of the leader. Having the right attitude can cause an increase in the performance of your employees.

In the movie *Remember the Titans*, there was a scene where the two defensive captains were arguing about the low performance of the football team. During their dispute, they brought up how different players on their team were not putting in any effort due to their differences in race.

Then one captain said, "Attitude reflects Leadership." When I heard this, I automatically had an aha moment. I, as the leader, set the tone for my team or organization.

If I go to work grumpy, my team will be grumpy. If I go to work sad, my team will be sad, but if I go to work with the right attitude, so will my team. It all starts with you; you have to tend to you first. What some people might call being selfish, I call it being selfless.

Because when you go to work with the right frame of mind, your employees will feed off of that. So, when we speak about emotional intelligence, it's all about self; self-awareness, self-regulation, self-motivation, self-management.

Having self-awareness or self-control helps you to understand why you do the things you do. It helps you to understand yourself. It brings awareness to our strengths and weaknesses. It helps us to be aware of our stressors and have effective communications with others.

Self-control is a wonderful thing; we must let the positive side build up. We must take the time to exercise the power we are given properly. All these things are needed to be a strong leader. We have to find a great balance; if we are unfair as a leader, it can cause disruptive culture.

Your employees want your E.N.E.R.G.Y when you come to work; they do not want a tired leader. ENERGY stands for Encouragement, Never Lie, Engagement, Recognition, Gratitude and Your Love.

Please, do not get me wrong; just because you have EQ does not make the leader effective. They must be able to have intelligence and adapt to organizational change and intense circumstances. Businesses are growing rapidly and trying to find ways to stay relevant.

I can remember when my platoon sergeants would come to me frustrated about changes in the unit and new soldiers in their platoons. They would come to my office, cursing up a storm. I would tell them to sit down and tell me exactly what the issue was.

I would let them vent about all they were dealing with. Then, after they would have gotten the anger all off their chest, I would give them my philosophy on new leadership new intent, and being a thermostat. I would tell them that not all higher echelons have the same intent. The main thing is you adapt; set the preferred temperature, but it has to be the right setting.

If you set the temperature too hot (mean, angry, and always yelling), then employees will want to quit or become resistant. If you set the temperature too cold (passive, indecisive and have a double standard), workers will quit or will try to take advantage of you.

See, when you understand the root cause of your emotions and how to use them, it can help you to effectively identify who you are and how you interact with others. You are in charge; people want to be led by a fearless leader. If you fold under pressure, you will lose your power base. Even when the road gets rough and you miss suspense, you will have to accept responsibility for the outcome as the leader. You cannot just accept it when everything goes in your favor.

Proverbs 18:21 says that life and death are in the power of the tongue. Proverbs 19:20 says, "listen to advice and accept instruction, that you may gain wisdom in the future." These two Scriptures are powerful for leaders when it comes to their influence. So, when under pressure, do not fold, you are stronger than you think. My advice to you is to learn from your mistakes and get better.

You may get knocked off balance and lose focus but never give in. Because in the end, whether you're a Senior leader, Pastor, Executive, Principal, or even a Head coach, you set the temperature for whatever room you are in.

Chapter 6

Motivating your Team

Any leader out there that says motivation is not important or doesn't work is full of crap. Motivation is needed to help your team go the extra mile. Notice how I said motivation and not money, although it is tempting and helps. This chapter is made to help you drive your employees with more than just money. I feel this is one of my strongest traits and something I enjoy.

You have to remain genuine behind your actions and be specific about your work and what you need completed. Make sure you always put out the right place and time of where to be or of the task and just keep a smile when doing it; trust me, it will take you pretty far.

At a particular time, I recall as a platoon sergeant during a training exercise on the Big Island of Hawaii; I was in charge of 65 personnel, enough people to just sit back and pull strings like a puppet. But that wasn't my leadership style; I believed in leading from the front.

Setting up the base was a team effort, which meant all hands-on deck. I sprang into action, assisting after giving the platoon my intent. I could never make my soldiers do anything that I was not willing to do myself.

I recalled setting up multiple tents from sunup till sundown that day. I overheard a group of my junior soldiers in the distance where they were smoking. One of them said, "I love working for Sergeant Jenkins; he motivates me."

"He is the only Sergeant First Class that I ever see working." Other soldiers in the group agreed. Workers do not learn from any manuals; they learn from the leader. The example we set is what they emulate.

Oliver Wendell Holmes said, "People can be divided into two classes: those who go ahead and do something, and those people who sit still and inquire, why wasn't it done the other way?"

Now, do not get me wrong; this does not work with all employees. Motivation is hard to sustain; you have to get to know your team and build a relationship. Another way to motivate your team is to create incentives.

Have rewards for certain things they do above standards. Developing a culture amongst your team or organization by being approachable helps, too. It's all about I, but I am not talking about one's self.

Let me break it down for you; one of the most important parts of a car is the battery. There is a connection between the engine and the battery. The car cannot start without the battery. If that battery runs dead, another dead battery cannot jump-start that dead battery. You have to charge the people under your supervision when they need a boost.

I am speaking about Influencing by spreading your passion for your work. Inspire those that cross your path and impact people to get results. By empowering your employees, you are doing all three. You should have a culture so headstrong that no one knows who the actual boss is. Always provide avenues for the workers' voices to be heard. When people love what they do, they will find a way to be heard.

It is up to you as the leader to instill purpose in others and make sure it is acted upon. Purpose provides practical ideas and turns them into concepts. Remember, Nehemiah lived under God's rule; he influenced and impacted his entire nation. His life modeled what it means to be a kingdom-minded person.

Chapter 7

Team Building

As a leader, you normally do not get to pick who your team is. You inherit a group of diverse individuals with different strengths and unique skill sets.

When building a team, I advise you to retain quality over quantity. I worked for a company where it was the other way around, and the culture was horrible. The moral was dry as the Mojave Desert, SMH, but the process is really simple, hire the right people, train them, and hold them accountable.

You must become the example you want to see from your team. You have to develop the self-discipline to do the right thing, even when no one is looking. My Brigade, CSM, shared a very important message with me from FM 22-100 (1990) "Be a Role Model." Whether you like it or not, you are on display at all times. Your actions say much more than your words.

Subordinates will watch you carefully and imitate your behavior. You must accept the obligation to be a worthy role model, and you cannot ignore the effect your behavior has on others. Implement guidelines, policies and procedures, but most of all, set goals with your team. I experienced an organization that did not hold its employees accountable.

The leadership picked and chose who they held accountable. Future leaders (employees) would see this and lose motivation, then grow a level of distrust. Knowing that my organization had this problem, I chose to address it. You have to professionally bring awareness to a situation that can affect or discredit the organization, team and you. You have to master conflict because it will happen, but they are necessary.

For most leaders, this is one of the toughest parts of the position. You have to be stern and not show favoritism. Your work relationship with your employees must remain professional and healthy. It is called LEADERship, not LIKERship. If you want to make everyone happy, do not be a leader, sell ice cream.

The goal is to be trustworthy and effective as a team. Gather your group and collectively discuss the best methods to accomplish the organization's intent as a team. There is so much we can learn from each other. Proverbs 27:17 says it best, "Iron sharpens Iron." This also helps to let your employees know their opinion matters.

Gospel singer, songwriter and Grammy award winner, Kirk Franklin, gave an analogy about getting results with experience using ingredients for a cake. In this analogy, he

29

spoke about how all the ingredients by themselves tasted horrible. He then asked the question, "Have you ever had cake?"

He describes how sweet cake is and how it uses all of those ingredients that are nasty together to make a cake. He speaks of the master chef (God) using the right amount of those ingredients (experience) when making the cake (results).

Let's use the same concept but dealing with a team. The leader who is the master chef brings a group of individuals (ingredients) together to work together and make something (cake) sweet. Without the leader, they would be ineffective alone.

On the next page, you can see an example of questions to talk about the needs of your team. Another great tool to use is the team-building cycle created by Bruce Tuckman. The cycle is to help identify problems as a group to come up with the best solution.

I also encourage using team-building events. Throughout my time as a team leader in the Army, I did monthly events with my soldiers. We did team bonding exercises and lunch-in, just to name a few. If you're looking for more ideas, you can find a lot of activities on my website (https://r2trisetothe-top.org) under tools.

Remember, teams that work great together give you the leader a sense of accomplishment. Teams that perform poorly leave us feeling frustrated and disappointed.

"The strength of the team is each individual member. The strength of each member is the team." --Phil Jackson

Examples of Questions to Ask Yourself

1. Is teamwork needed for your team to accomplish its goals?

2. Is the team's role in the organization clear?

3. Does the team have the resources it needs to accomplish its goals?

4. Does the organization's culture encourage teamwork?

5. How effective is the leadership in the team?

6. Are team members motivated to help the team achieve its goals?

Chapter 8

Goal Setting

Setting goals are like reading a map; you have this picture of where you want to be. Certain places are farther than others, which means it will take longer to get there. Something that a map and goals have in common is that "ALL" destinations are achievable.

Why do we say "no problem, we can do that" when it comes to going on vacation or visiting family and friends, but when it comes to the goals we set, we talk ourselves out of doing it? Nowadays, we use more technologies, like GPS, to get to our destinations.

This is what I call a coach or mentor, a person who advises you on steps to take to reach your goals — someone who holds you accountable and does not let you make wrong turns.

During Operation Iraqi Freedom (OIF 8-9), I read this book by Stephen R. Covey, "The Seven Habits of Highly Effective People". The book changed my life in so many ways, especially when it came to my influence. It helped me realize what I could and could not control. I learned about prioritizing my life for personal change.

In this book, there was a chapter that discussed roles and goals. It said once you've identified your role then you can start setting goals. The goal I set was to become an asset to my unit. Now, during this time, I was a section chief working night shift with only eight soldiers. After applying what I read, my section's production increased, and my platoon sergeant was impressed. I was switched to day shift; implanted the same structure and direction that I did during my time working nights, and it "WORKED!"

At this time, my First Sergeant noticed a change in operations and requested for me to take the position of becoming the platoon sergeant. I was nervous because I would be in charge of 63 soldiers instead of eight — "HUGE" increase of responsibility in such a short amount of time. I was thankful for the opportunity; I accepted the challenge, and just like that, Goal Achieved.

By identifying my role for my life (Section Chief), selecting important people for that role, as my employees, I wrote a number of goals for my role that are in line with my employees.

Then I did something roughly every week to make progress in that role. I challenged myself every Monday, asking what are you going to do to make a difference for the better?

Trust me, this will influence others to become greater than you imagined.

Proverbs 29:18 says, "Where there is no vision, the people perish: but he that keepeth the law, happy is he."

In the Army, when we go before a promotion board, we have to prepare a packet that has all our personal and military information in it to present to the board members. It was highly encouraged that when we write our biography, that we put our long and short-term goals in it.

Let's be honest, coming through the ranks, you never really had regards for writing out your goals. But by separating your goals like this, it will help you to achieve them. Completing your short-term goals will build your confidence to continue striving for the long-term goals.

Your short-range goals are for tomorrow, something you can achieve less than a year. Your long-term goals are your dreams, what you inspire to be, or do.

The Lord said to write the vision and make it plain on tablets, so he may run who reads it. He also said if it seems slow, WAIT for it; it will surely come, Habakkuk 2:2-3. Writing down your goals means that you can visually see them. So, by using the technique, SMART goals, you can narrow down and achieve realistic goals. It is an acronym that stands for Specific, Measurable, Achieve, Realistic, and Time.

- Specific: The Who and what of your goal. Exactly what you want to achieve.

- Measurable: How can you measure the process, quantify?

- Achieve: Do you have everything needed to make this happen? If not, then what is missing?

- Realistic: Is it practical or true to life?

- Time: When do you plan to have this accomplished, a deadline?

By having these goals outlined helps to provide direction for you and your team. When leaders give a clear intent of what their priorities are, it makes jobs easier for staff to make sound judging decisions.

"Shoot for the moon. Even if you miss, you'll land among the stars." –Les Brown

Conclusion

I believe trapped inside of all of you, are leadership traits of great importance. This does not mean everyone should be a leader. Overall, you have to find your purpose. Again, you have to make a serious decision to develop the leader within you.

Great leadership is needed everywhere. Businesses are faced with unique and unprecedented challenges. Having leadership in place helps to meet organizational goals. All companies need effective and sustainable leaders.

Words from the wise, being just a manager just doesn't cut it anymore for any organization. Businesses, homes, schools, lives are all suffering from the lack of leadership. You can help change that situation.

If the results of your family, team, or organization are not pleasing to you, then apply these principles that are outlined in this book, which have all been proven to work if put to use. This book was not only made for organizational purposes but to also challenge you and ignite the leader in you.

Instead of always looking for the person who is out front, let's look within ourselves. We all can affect people and influence them. Things won't change overnight; you, as the leader, have to be patient, committed, vulnerable and coachable.

Being coachable is a very important trait that doesn't take talent. Even if you aren't an athlete, being coachable is one of life's most valuable skills. By doing this, you're making yourself vulnerable for improvement. If you wish to grow or become better, you have to be open to feedback.

Part of being coachable is having the right attitude. The military taught me that my job as a leader was to train, teach, coach and mentor. Having a great coach can really increase your chances of success and bring the best out of you.

Coaches should be willing to invest and equip you with all the resources needed to be a greater you. During my deployment in Arifjan, Kuwait, I would have multiple leaders come to me complaining about what was wrong with the company. Every time they came with a problem, I would ask them for a solution. 85 percent of the time, they had no suggestions.

After having a long dialogue with my commander, he suggested I lead an eight-week leadership workshop. We conducted group work, open discussion, scenarios, written and hands-on based training. We wanted for all the leaders in our organization to be successful in leading their formations.

Having those workshops help take an objective look at an individual's strengths and weaknesses in all areas of their life. Of course, you're not going to get everyone's full participation, but for those you do reach, the feeling is unimaginable.

I would always tell the soldiers after training to learn it, digest it and apply it. You, as the leader, have to contribute to your own success. If you're not willing to step outside of your comfort zone, there is a possibility that you will be in the same place you were.

Without commitment, you will never start; it means taking on an obligation greater than yourself. I vowed to myself that I would become devoted to my family, loyal to the people under my charge, and an asset to my organization. You have to have made up your mind that you're in it for the long haul. Be someone that people can count on.

As a leader, there will always be times where you don't feel like being a leader. That's when you have to be steadfast and unmovable and stay the course. Pull yourself together and say "I AM" going to do the hard, right instead of the easier wrong. Commitment is where we achieve great accomplishments. During my military career, I endured setbacks time and time again.

I did not give up; I fought the good fight, day after day when the pressure hits. No matter how tired, depressed, or whatever adversity I was going through. I never showed it. I was disciplined, I held myself accountable to a higher standard. I was committed, I trusted the process and never quit.

I know the stigma of being vulnerable as a leader is being weak. This is something we all experience and it's completely normal. We, as leaders, make it seem like we do not experience trauma or that we have it all together when we don't. Even Superman had to be Clark Kent sometime. So, think of it as vulnerability as kryptonite think of it as a superpower. They say that some of the most trusted leaders were vulnerable to their employees. Leadership is not easy, yet it is the most rewarding profession you will ever have.

I think the King of Pop said it best, and I quote, "If You Want To Make The World A Better Place, Take A Look At "YOURSELF" And Make A Change." I am here to tell you that you're losing money if you are not using leadership.

"The quality of tomorrow's leaders lies in the character of today's leaders-in-training." Dr. Myles Monroe

About the Author

Sylvester Jenkins III

Sylvester is a native of Columbus, Ga. He is a combat veteran with four tours in Iraq and one tour in Afghanistan. He has completed 21 years of military service in the US Army. He has accomplished measurable results under extreme pressure while leading teams of multiple personnel in a dynamic, fast-paced environment. Sylvester possesses a comprehensive background in Training & Development and Policy Implementation, derived from conducting domestic and global operations. He managed risk upon multiple lines to protect assets, property, and equipment valued over $5 million while meeting the expectations of senior leadership. Sylvester possesses extensive knowledge in Strategic Planning, Data Analysis, and Program Management. He is a recipient of multiple awards for outstanding performance and professionalism. Sylvester is a member of the National Society of Leadership and Success. He graduated from Columbia Southern University, where he received his Bachelor of Science in Organizational Leadership in 2016. He is an experienced leader who has empowered 100's of people by helping them reach their goals, both personally and professionally. Sylvester is married to Denise Jenkins and they are blessed with four children - Emmanuel, Da'Shun, Alex and Rileigh.

Made in the USA
Coppell, TX
18 January 2020